MW01672256

Alycia Bruce

BookLeaf Publishing

Presentation by *BookLeaf Publishing*

Web: www.bookleafpub.com

E-mail: info@bookleafpub.com

ISBN: 9789395969291

First edition 2022

DEDICATION

This book is dedicated to the lost and lonely, the misfits, the outcasts; the little girls with big dreams and tender, paper hearts.

ACKNOWLEDGEMENT

I think this quote by Mindy Copeland says it best, "Anything is possible when you have the right people there to support you."

This book and its publication would not have been possible without the love and support of my friends and family. There are so many people that have contributed to this: My sister Emily: who receives and reads the first draft of every poem, Jules: who gives me the courage to reach for impossible dreams, and Grace: my soul-sister, who makes me feel safe, sane, and seen, and everyone else who gave me a safe space to feel vulnerable and share my art.

PREFACE

From the moment I learned to read I have always found comfort in the words of others. In middle school; I began to find my own words, my voice through writing.

During a particularly tough time in my life, to step out of my comfort zone, I shared a poem that I had written and the response was instantaneous. Not only were people hearing and understanding me in a way they never had before, but my poems were resonating with them. I had become a voice like the ones before me.

This lit a fire under me, and I began writing and sharing my poetry on my Facebook page before I knew it, I had a large body of work ready to be shared, in time with a larger audience. After a lot of soul-searching, I ultimately decided now is the right time to take this leap.

Birthright

I know I'm supposed to feel something: a little heartbroken, a bit of remorse.

But, all I keep thinking about is karma, and how it's about time that you're finally getting yours.

I won't pretend that I've forgotten; I won't absolve you of your sin.

Jesus may still love you, but we all know I'm not enough like him.

I wouldn't even pretend to mourn you after you're dead and gone.

Because the cycle that you started, is one that still lives on.

It's in the knife under my pillow.

It's in the hangers on the door.

It's in these violent shivers coursing down my spine, as silent shadows sneak across the floor.

It’s in the pill bottles filling up the counter.

It’s in the nightlight by my bed.

It’s the fractured relationship with my mother.

It’s the way I drown in my own head.

That’s why I couldn’t even make it through a funeral, surrounded by our broken family, while unenlightened members of your congregation line up to commend you for your legacy.

I know what you gave to the world.

I know the birthright you left me.

Legacy

We haven't spoken in a while.

Guess there's not much left to say.

I can't fake another smile, just to get you through another day.

You're haunted in the midnight hours, by all these choices that you've made.

And I may be made in your image, but I won't be making your mistakes.

The sins of a mother passed down from yesterday…a shadow of a father, a ghost that never truly fades.

Time's flown out the window, and we can't get it back.

The only thing you're missing is what we've never had.

There's always been this distance, a chasm in between, the people that we are and who we want to be.

And, it does not make a difference, the ending stays the same.

That's always been our legacy, much more than a last name.

We are getting nowhere with this constant back-and-forth, there's nothing left I haven't tried, to finally end this war.

The time has come to put my sword down.

I'm giving up this fight, leaving it up to fate, putting our past behind.

There's no fighting history, it's all in the blood.

It's always been our destiny, to destroy the ones we love.

I'm just a product of my raising: both the apple and the tree.

No, I wasn't borne from something healthy, but something healthy has to come from me.

For the sake of my future children and the love I'm still praying to find, I have to sacrifice your hearts to keep from breaking mine.

This Noble Sacrifice

If I said I didn't miss you, I'd be lying through
my teeth.

But, if someone has to hurt here, then I'll make
sure it's me.

Cut myself wide open, just so you don't have to
bleed.

Just turn away now, this really isn't something
you want to see.

Is it masochistic, am I just a martyr, or simply
the little lamb you've raised for the slaughter?

My will ain't free, I've never had choices.

It's not up to me, just you and these voices in my
head.

And isn't that love, this noble sacrifice?

The way I fight like hell to keep you sheltered,
leave the wool over your eyes.

For better, for worse, my steps they don't falter.

Forever curiously cursed, your damned and
dutiful daughter.

I'll always wonder which you built first: the
cradle or the altar.

In My Daddy's Shoes

My daddy didn't raise a quitter.

But, he didn't raise me, at all.

So if I've been led by his example, I'm gonna claim it's not my fault.

Guess it's true, the apple never really falls far from the tree.

And even those with the best intentions, only bring out the worst in me.

I'll never make it easy.

Baby, loving me is hard.

I've got a stubborn streak a country mile wide.

I'll never let down my guard.

Cause I'm the picture of perfection, as long as you can't see the scars.

I won't show you mine, but, I can cause a few of my own.

Cause when the going gets tough, hell, I'm already gone.

If it's fight or flight, there's really no question, which path I'll always choose.

I run away a little faster, in my daddy's shoes.

Hurricane

You taught me when to run, and showed me how to hide.

You couldn't teach me to heal, from the pain we share inside.

You never taught me to read, or how to ride a bike, but, you taught me how to leave, and God knows that I've tried.

How can I walk away, when you're always a step behind?

Though if I tried to reach for you, a shadow's all I'd find.

Am I the worst of me, or just the best of you?

Is there anything left standing, by the time our hurting's through?

Chaos and devastation, follow in my path.

And no one lives to see, the me beyond the mask.

But you are not to blame, for all the pretty things I break.

I am my own hurricane, not a storm left in your wake.

Turning Out Like You

You couldn't choose me.

You never did.

What kind of mother doesn't want her kids?

And leaves them to grow up on their own?

My worst fear is that I turn out like you.

That's why I live my life the way I do, so guarded and alone.

Then I blame the world, I blame you, I blame myself.

Cause I can't help but hate you when I can't love somebody else.

Sometimes, I think I'm slowly getting better.

The future's finally coming clear.

But, another couple drinks, another sleepless night, and I see your eyes inside my mirror.

And then I run, just like my father.

Just like I said I would never do.

Call me a hypocrite, but I'd rather risk, turning into him, than turning out like you.

You know, if things were different if nothing were the same…

I would have myself a family of my own, with my eyes and his last name.

But, that's not happening right now, and that future, it may never be.

Not until the day I can look into my mirror, and be certain that my reflection, is the only one staring back at me.

Ends With Me

Mother, can you see it now?

The writing's on the wall.

Tell me, do you feel it, how the devil's come to call?

The time has come for reaping, all these careless seeds you've sown.

Realizing your worst fear, you're waking up alone.

Mama, come and get your lover; he's creeping in my room.

I'm scared, shaking under the covers; you said you'd be home soon.

Mommy, now I'm waking, aching, shattered in the night.

Can't stop these tears from falling, and you won't meet my eyes.

He's there at the table, and watching TV on the couch.

How can you pretend you don't know, you let a monster in the house?

Mother, I'm all grown up now, not a soul to call my own.

Still shrouded in your shadow, and waking up alone.

I've made peace with most of my demons, except the ones that share your face.

Endless nights I lie awake and wonder, how the hell we've gotten to this place?

You: everyone's favorite victim; me: another careless casualty.

Though that's always worked for you, that is never who I want to be.

I need to find a way to exorcise this anger, let it go, find some peace, stop subsisting in this silence, and finally get some sleep.

There'll be friends to gather around my table, and laughter on my couch, no more living with these demons; only love shared in my house.

No longer just your fallen apple, I am a whole damn tree.

And even if I have to burn the entire forest to the ground; this cycle ends with me.

Blood and Bone

You're a stranger to me, though we are blood and bone.

The things you did to me, at night and all the times we were alone...

I was left a shell, a shadow; your ghost, it haunts me still.

And I know it's been a lifetime, but I still can't shake these pills.

They're a crutch, a lifeline, but they help me through the night.

I know you can't relate, I'm sure you sleep alright.

I see you've got a little girl now, I'm sure with stories of her own.

And her mama can't figure out, why she won't sleep alone.

"There's no monster here, babe. Now let daddy tuck you in."

And she'll wonder through the years, when did it all begin?

Is there something that she missed?

Was there writing on the wall?

Monsters do exist.

And you're one of the worst ones of them all.

I wish I could say I didn't wish you ill, but that would be a lie.

Cause I hope you rot in Hell, and I pray for you to die.

I'll be there at your graveside with Champagne and a smile.

They say I really should forgive, but that's just never been my style.

I have a thirst for blood; a need for justice to be served.

And I just won't feel satisfied. until you get what you deserve.

Rediscovering Me

I close my eyes against the shadows.

I shudder every time the wind blows.

Every footstep in the hallway, I think it's coming my way.

With every creak across the floor, in every rattle of a door, all my nightmares come to life; I know that he'll come back each time.

So I'm, looking over my shoulder, checking under my bed, this girl I don't know her, she is not who I am.

I used to dance in the moonlight, but now I'm shying from the sunset.

Silent tears fall from my bloodshot eyes, my fourth drink hasn't hit me yet.

And sleep, it don't come easy; can't let my senses leave me.

It's dark on the inside; there is nowhere I can hide when my demons come to greet me.

They take my hand, they pull me in, they scream "Welcome back, old friend! "

But, we're not friends, we're just familiar, and I can't find the will to escape.

So, why run from fate?

I bow down, admit defeat, I surrender, I concede, to their hold over me.

I sink fast, I sink low, and it starts to feel like home.

Down here among the broken, echoes the secrets left unspoken; my screams go unheard and the pain, it feels deserved.

And I'm not looking over my shoulder, not checking under my bed.

This girl, I don't know her, but she's become who I am; she's shattered and she's faithless, lost herself, though she is blameless.

It's here that she finds rest, among the damned and the depressed.

No longer looking for a saving grace; she's found her place.

But, there's only so long someone can hide themselves away, sometimes it's wrong to stay where you feel safe.

The darkness starts to smother, each breath coming weaker than the other.

It's time to rise and let the truth be uncovered.

And I'm not afraid to stand back up, not ashamed to call it what it was.

I found myself, I fought to breathe, defeated the demons inside of me.

I'm not looking over my shoulder, not checking under my bed.

This girl, I think I know her, she reminds me of who I am.

She's riddled with flaws but she's alive; been through Hell and she survived.

She's let go of her past, she's finally free.

Learning to live, learning to love, learning to be, getting to know myself again; rediscovering me.

Hypocrite

You don’t get to pick at my scars when you've ignored the gaping wounds.

You’re not allowed to weigh in on my method of healing, as if you’ve never walked in my shoes.

I am continually changing.

There’s always more work for me to do.

I know I have never been perfect but, then again, neither have you.

You try to hide the sinful secrets of the family home, as you gather ‘round the table.

Sweep it all under the rug.

But, there’s no way you’ll be able, to wash the blood out from the floorboards and all the cracks up in between, as you swallow down another dinner and all the bullshit apologies you know that they’ll never truly mean.

Your silence is complicity.

You've been an accomplice to every crime committed.

So, don't you dare sit there in judgment of the way I chose to deal with the aftermath of the hand that I've been given.

You have to be a certain kind of hypocrite to have the nerve to throw stones from that fucking horror house you live in.

Don't Let me Sleep Alone

When I sleep, let me sleep soundly.

If I must wake, let me see the world through different eyes.

One moment in between, to touch the boundary, to rest between the Earth and sky.

I just need that time... A few seconds of space to breathe, another chance to change my mind, a reason to believe.

The night is closing in, the air grows colder still.

So many things I'd left to do; now, I guess I never will.

You may think I've given up.

Trust me, there is no easy way out.

You listened to the whispers, you couldn't hear me shout.

Our 60 seconds are up.

There are decisions to be made, I thought this was what I wanted...

What I wouldn't trade, to rewrite my story. just go back and right the wrong, to take back all these choices, and change the ending to my last song.

I. AM. NOT. READY.

Not ready to stop singing.

Not ready to quit breathing.

I'm begging you to wake me from this nightmare that I'm weaving.

Be the light in my dark tunnel, be the hand that guides me home, a friendly face on a crowded highway...

Just don't let me sleep alone.

Saved By Grace

I'm screaming, but you can't hear me.

I'm breathing, just barely.

I'm reaching out blindly in this fog.

On trembling knees, I've fought an endless battle.

Suspended here on this tightrope I straddle, between the Earth and sky.

With shaking hands, I stand with waning will, in the place where time stands still.

Will I fall or will I fly?

Seconds again start to tick slowly by, as I contemplate my earth and sky, I feel the time grow nigh.

Time to fall or time to fly?

With every passing moment, I start to slip, trying to hold on to hope but I'm losing my grip on reality, still, no one comes for me.

Then, piercing through the dark, I saw her shining face.

I pled, "You're too pure, you must leave this place."... "I must stay. No, I'm not that strong; it's clear you've gotten it all wrong."

She said, "You may leave, no longer toil, go on, return to the mortal coil. There are people there who need you so. My dear, it's not your time to go. Your friends are waiting, and for the rest of your life there'll be no more struggle, there'll be no strife."

It was then I knew without a doubt, she was sent to pull me out.

I looked again at her smiling face and knew at once, I'd been saved by Grace.

Peter Pan

(For Ben. Forever.)

You called me Tinker Bell.

I guess that makes you Peter Pan.

A boy who'll stay a boy forever, flown away to Neverland.

You always burned too brightly.

It's true you belong there among the clouds.

But, I am just here wondering, if you're ever planning to come down.

Come and fill this hollow; your shadow lingers in empty rooms.

With a needle and some thread, we could have you fixed up soon.

Your sisters miss you dearly.

For your mother time stands still.

Surrounded by your echo, in this space, no one else could ever fill.

Your lost boys need their leader; they crow till they grow hoarse.

Is there really no reason to turn your ship around, no benevolent wind to right your course?

I'm struggling to understand, this word that is goodbye, just like the word forever, and how there are still so many tears to cry.

I guess I'll never know, why a life is ended when it feels like it's only just began.

What good is fairy magic, if nothing ever goes to plan?

Thank you for the laughter, the adventures, and the fun.

But although we're still not ready, your time with us and on this earth is done.

I'll always think of you fondly when I look up at the sky.

And maybe someday, someday when I'm older, I'll learn to say goodbye.

Pieces

I was living in denial.

Our pieces didn't fit.

And so I started changing mine, bit by broken bit.

I softened up my edges; you found me so unpolished.

And darlin', I'd do anything just to get acknowledged.

At long last, I had you, but much to my vexation, I
never earned your love, just your fleeting fascination.

Your eyes, scorched my skin, as I danced across the
floor.

The words you whispered made me shiver, and
always left me wanting more.

You were happy to share my bed, but to share
yourself would be a crime.

And so we lay there, frozen together, each of us
choking on the sands of time.

You: too fearful to move forward, me: too tired of
holding back.

I'd always kept my heart locked up like a fortress, but those three small words slipped through the cracks.

I have to tell you, baby, I've never seen someone more afraid.

I tried to take them back, and clean up the mess I made.

But the damage had been done, I'd shown my cards too fast.

In the blink of an eye, somehow, our future has become our past.

I still think of you sometimes, when I look up at the stars.

My first love, my first heartbreak, now I share your ugly scars.

I know that I shouldn't have changed for you, those pieces that never fit.

And so I've started fixing them, bit by broken bit.

B. (Pieces Part 2)

I'm waking up alone, in bed, holding you close.

Haunted by all these questions, with the answers I'll never know.

I knew we shouldn't have done it, we took it too far.

Years of friendship down the drain, for moments stolen in the dark.

With everything that's been taken, I learned to hold on hard, and though you're the one that got away, I still have my scars.

I miss your smile, all those times we laughed, the way you knew just what I needed, without me having asked.

It ain't easy, this moving on, and it's hard to face the mirror when I remember why you're gone.

And I don't blame you, I know you tried.

But darlin', nothing was going to save us, from these tears I had to cry.

I couldn't be your first, love, but thank you for being mine, and leaving all the pieces when you left me behind.

One day he'll find me and the pieces, they'll finally fit, but today, I'm going to lie here with a ghost and pretend for a little bit.

I'm going to edit our story, rewrite and change the end, so I can wake up in the morning and still call you my friend.

Last Words

Those words that you spoke, are still tangled in my head.

Still waking cold, with your ghost in my bed.

Still talking to the moon, still trying to move the stars, still holding on to you, though I don't even know where you are.

And, if I can't even recall the feeling of your touch, then tell me how my foolish heart has me convinced that I still miss you this much.

They say when you love something, you've just got to set it free; but I hope from time to time you'll think of me.

And I hope you love her like I once hoped you'd love me...

And that she's everything to you that I was always trying to be.

I pray you find it, your inner peace, and the demons they don't keep you up at night and she's the only reason you lose sleep.

Once my lost boy, with her you'll make your home.

And I pray you'll never know this heartache of waking up alone.

Don't ya worry bout me, darlin'.

I've heard that time heals old wounds.

Someday, I'll break this spell you've wrapped around me.

Someday, I'll forget you hung the moon.

I'll stop fucking with the stars.

I'll stop holding your words and drowning in the dark.

Move The Stars

We were both lying in my bed.

I couldn't look at you.

You kept trying to turn my head.

That was the moment that I knew, you knew.

So, I decided to take a chance.

Throw my wishes to the stars.

The night I felt safest in your hands, that's when it all just fell apart.

I often wonder now, "Where would we be, if our roles had been reversed?

If I'd have let you chase me down, if I'd have made you kiss me first?

Would I have died in that town?

Would we be married or divorced right now?

And if we had a couple kids, would they have your eyes or mine?

Could we have countered all their curses?

Uprooted the trees?

Could we have raised something beautiful out of the ashes of such an ugly, forgotten tragedy?"

I know that the universe has its own plans.

What's meant to be, will always come to be.

Although I liked the picture at the time, there was always a bigger one in store that I just couldn't see.

Try as I might, I could never find a way to move the stars.

But, I am eternally grateful to know, that they were always moving me.

The Captor and the Key

And I, can't deal with uncertainty, don't do too well with apologies, don't know how to make things right.

Try to start a conversation, it always ends in confrontation.

I just can't see the other side.

Seems it's always one step forward and three steps back, but this stubborn pride is all I have.

It don't keep me warm, it doesn't fit quite right.

Still, it's her and I, alone again tonight.

I know whose to blame; I know I built these walls.

But, why take the leap when there's no safe space to fall?

Where once were wings, see these angry scars.

Caught in a cell of my own creation, watching
life go on without me through the bars.

And no, you can not free me, though I know you
may want to help.

Both the captor and the key, the answers lie only
within myself.

No More Time To Waste

And I can't say, how that little girl's become the stranger standing in my mirror.

I try in vain to search the shadows in her eyes, but the truth is, the answers aren't coming any clearer.

All the things I couldn't have, still keep me up at night.

All the missteps and mistakes, too late to make them right.

I can not slow the sands of time, I can not bind the hands of fate.

But, if I could just rewind, I'd go back to those days, when my dreams were far too big, and this world wonderful and wide.

This ain't the life I'm meant live; just a role I'm trapped inside.

And her shoes, they don't fit, and her smile's not quite right.

Can't find my motivation.

Tell me, what's my line?

Someone close the curtain, let me take my final bow, step off of this stage, and wipe the makeup from my brow.

I thank y'all for watching, really hope you enjoyed the show.

But, now it's time to stop this charade, now I've got to go, where my dreams aren't quite as big but they're something I can hold, still a world I'm trying to conquer, so many tales I've left untold.

This is the life I choose to live; no matter how long it may take.

I will find my own horizon, a new dawn's gonna break out of this darkness, find the flame within my eyes.

The time has come to discover the woman I truly am, cast away the old disguise.

And I welcome the change of every season and the guiding hand of fate.

No more waiting, no more pretending, no more time to waste.

Reign

I fear the slumbering giant I have buried deep within.

A living, breathing parasite, it writhes beneath my skin.

Weaving wicked path from my head straight to my heart, armed with a million vicious lies designed to tear my world apart.

They undermine my confidence, piece by piece they tear me down.

And though I am my own jailer, these shackles still hold me, bound.

It seems so simple, really, from the outside looking in.

The reflection in the mirror is the same as it's always been.

I see the same blue eyes, though maybe the light inside has faded; this smile seems foreign though: callous, brittle, jaded.

Sometimes, I catch a glimpse of the woman I want to be.

She is achingly familiar.

I am her and she is me; it's plain as the nose upon my own face.

In just a second, an instant...another takes her place.

There's a stranger staring back at me; reveling in my defeat, stealing each breath from my lungs, poisoning my every heartbeat.

Someday, I'll be the woman that hides inside the mirror.

Once I find that elusive key, I'll be free and clear.

A prisoner no longer, I will break this chain.

I will slay my own dragon.

A new queen will reign.

Someone Worth Melting For

I've been a fighter, not a lover, since the time that I was small.

Everything that seemed ripe to ruin me; somehow, I made it through it all.

Burning bridges, slamming doors, safe up in my ivory tower.

But, the one cold hard truth that can not be ignored?

The ice queen gets no flowers.

Heavy is the head that wears the crown.

Arctic eyes and armored heart.

I have to believe, there's still time to change me.

I wouldn't even know quite where to start.

Men want women: soft like springtime, smiles, warm like the sun.

Not a soldier in a sundress; not a rebel, born to run.

How can I fight against my own nature, thaw these glaciers so deeply rooted in my bones?

Though this haven has kept me sheltered, I was never meant to wither here alone.

Where there are bars, I will create a window; where there are walls, I'll build a door.

There is a world of possibilities out there, just waiting for me.

And, although there is no map to my future or blueprints for what the universe may have in store…

I'm ready to start living life again, split this guarded heart wide open, and finally find myself, someone worth melting for.

Printed in the USA
CPSIA information can be obtained
at www.ICGtesting.com
LVHW010212180224
772058LV00004B/424

9 789395 969291